FLOW:
Adventures at
Prosperity Patch

by Kim D. H. Butler
and Spencer Shaw

Prosperity Economics Movement
22790 Highway 259 South
Mount Enterprise, TX 75681
www.ProsperityEconomics.org

First Edition
ISBN: 979-8-9940994-2-1 (paperback)

Produced in the United States of America

Published with the assistance of Social Motion Publishing, which specializes in books that benefit causes and nonprofits. For more information, go to SocialMotionPublishing.com.

Acknowledgments

I love animals; I have had dogs, cats, chickens, pigs, sheep, goats, and dairy cows since 4th grade, and now I have Alpacas! I also love Prosperity Thinking. Now, I am excited to share these loves with children of all ages through my third love: reading! Whether you are an adult or have children, grandchildren, or great-grandchildren, reading with others (and playing games too!) is a fabulous bonding experience, and I am so grateful to the team of Spencer and family for bringing it to your table.

Enjoy, Kim Butler, Mount Enterprise, TX

I grew up hearing stories from my dad and kinfolk which shaped my world today. Sharing stories with kids is a fun way to help them think about big dreams. Huge thank you to my wife for leading our homeschooling and our kids for listening to these stories. A big thank you to Emma for helping Kim and I feel like children again.

We are so grateful to everyone who helps us make this book, like Amanda who leads this project and our awesome designers Cy and Holly.

Spencer Shaw

One sunny day at Prosperity Patch, Emma, the wise Great Dane, noticed the swings and slides at the farm were looking old and a bit unsafe.

She gathered her friends under the big oak tree and shared her idea.

"Our playground needs new equipment. Why don't we start a lemonade stand to raise the money?" Emma suggested.

The other pets loved the idea and quickly pooled their savings to buy lemons, sugar, and cups.

Miguel the Bull, strong and dependable, was in charge of the budget.

"We've spent some of our money on these supplies," he explained.

"Now let's sell some lemonade and make more money to buy new playground gear!"

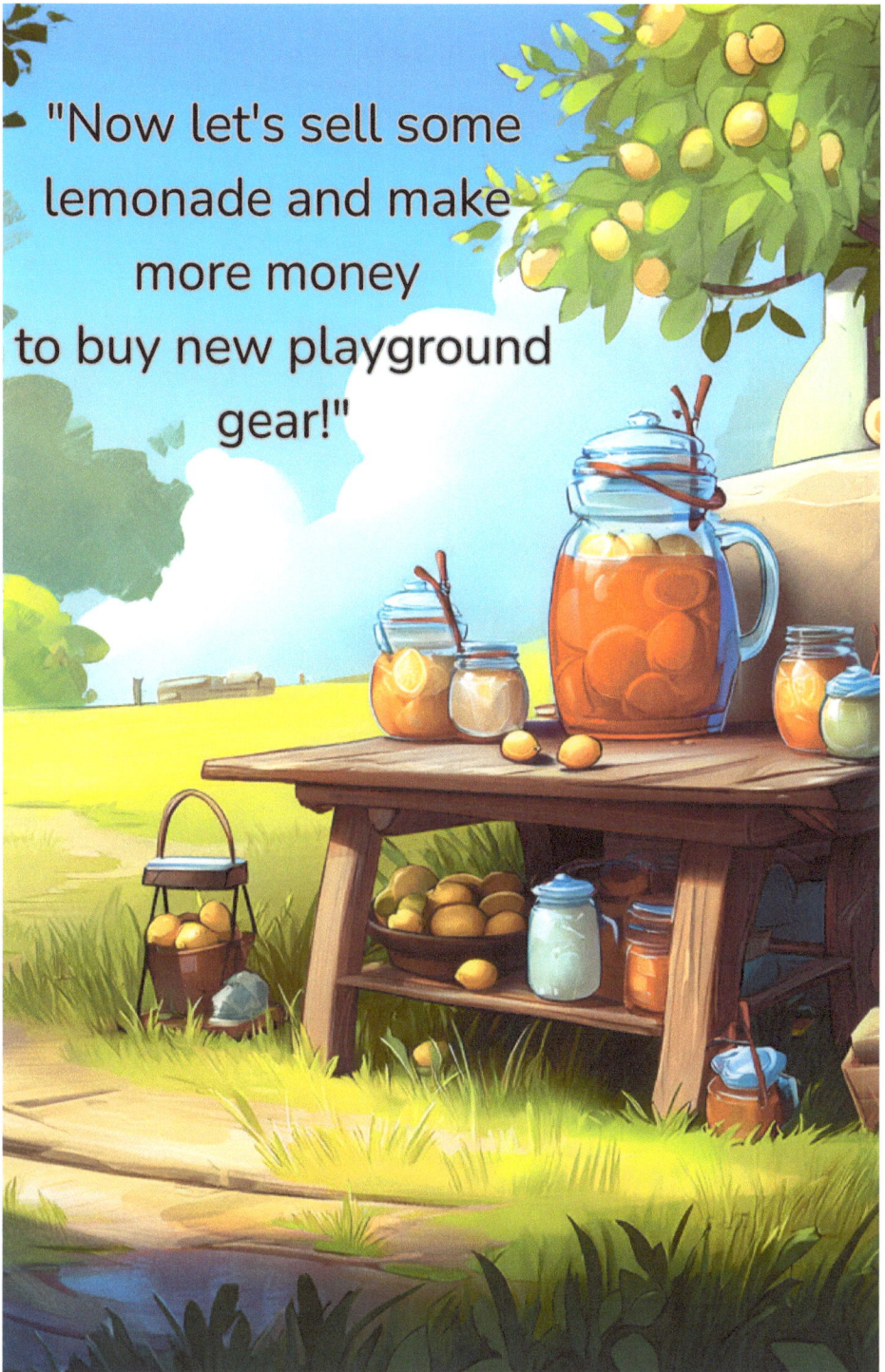

Their lemonade stand was a big hit at first. Visitors loved their sweet, refreshing drink.

But soon, they faced some challenges. The weather turned rainy, which meant fewer customers. Then, a new lemonade stand opened nearby, offering cheaper lemonade.

Zippy the Rabbit had an idea. "Let's use cheaper ingredients to save money and lower our prices," he suggested.

They tried it, but their lemonade didn't taste as good anymore. Their customers noticed and their interest faded.

Worried, Emma decided to ask the farmer for advice. "Keeping your lemonade tasty and managing your money wisely is key," he told them.

"Picture your piggy bank as a magical treasure box. Coins and bills go in when you save and come out when you buy things.

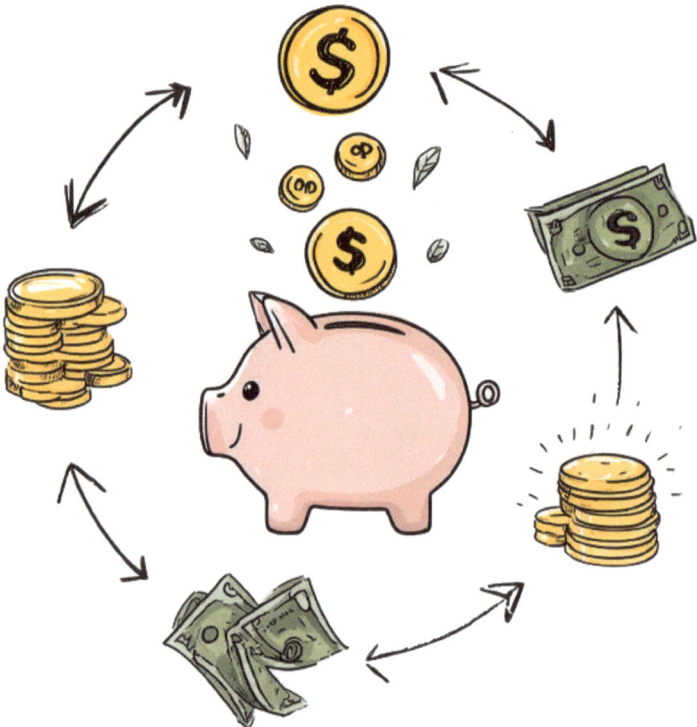

Just like a seesaw, you want to keep it steady so your treasure box stays full of goodies!"

With a new understanding, the pets changed their plan.

Peanut the Cat created a special deal: buy ten lemonades, get one free.

Kid the Alpaca helped by telling everyone about their yummy lemonade.

They also decided to spend some of their earnings on improving their lemonade stand.

They added colorful signs and comfy seating, which made more people stop by.

Their new strategies worked! Their lemonade stand became popular again. The money started flowing in steadily, and they were able to save enough for new playground equipment.

The day they installed the new swings and slides, all the pets felt proud.

They had learned a lot about running a business and managing money.

Emma's Advice:

Hey there Prosperity friends! Imagine you have a magic jar. Every time you get money, put it in the jar. Now, decide how much you want to save and how much you want to spend.

This plan helps you see where your money is going! Sometimes, we have to choose between things we need and things we want.

Managing your money wisely helps you get what you need and save for the things you really want. Happy saving!

Emma's Questions:

1. What are some fun things you can do instead of buying new toys to save your money?
2. Can you think of a special place where you would like to keep your money safe?
3. How can you decide what is important to buy, or if you should save your money?
4. What is something you would like to save your money for in the future, like a special toy or a fun day out?
5. How can you earn money at home working on special tasks?

A note for your parents!

As our thank-you, the QR code below will give you a valuable white paper focused on Income Strategies at ProsperityEconomics.org/permission.